Learn**English**
WithAfrica

Learn English With Africa

A2 Short Stories in English

(Vol. 1)

Beginner Level

By
Thandi Ngwira Gatignol

CONTENTS

FOREWORD

This is a collection of ten beginner short stories that are easy to read and understand. The stories are all set in Africa and they feature a wide range of interesting characters and themes.

You will find motivational short stories as well as entertaining ones. Some of the short stories will stir your imagination and some of them will surprise you with their humour and unexpected situations.

<u>Tips for getting the most out of a short story</u>
First, pay attention to the meaning of the story before focusing on grammatical structures.

Then, read the short story again and ask yourself the following questions: 1) What is the story about? 2) Who are the characters and what are their motivations? 3) What is the difference between the beginning of the short story and the end?

Lastly, write down interesting words, expressions or grammatical structures so that you can review them later. You will thus build your vocabulary and improve your English grammar in an active way.

I hope that this first collection of beginner short stories meets your expectations and fosters your own creativity.

Thandi Ngwira Gatignol, Founder and Author (Learn English With Africa)

The Old Witch and the Wish

(with Wishes Vocabulary)

I am not afraid of the old woman who greets me each time I meet her when I am on my way to school. Most of my friends are. I don't know why. She always smiles at me when she sees me. I think she is very friendly and I would like to know where she lives.

"Good morning my son," she says.

"Good morning *agogo*. How are you today?"

"I am fine; I am fine, thank you. What a lovely boy you are…now hurry up, my son. You don't want to miss your bus, do you?"

My friends say I should never talk to her. Rumour has it that she is a witch. She is said to fly at night. I don't know if anybody has ever seen her do that. Limbani, my best friend, says I should avoid her at all costs.

"That woman is childless. She has no family and she always talks to strangers. Sometimes she insults them without any reason at all. There is something wrong with her. Charles, you should never talk to anyone who is shunned by everybody. It brings bad luck. I wish you would just listen to me."

Maybe my friends are right. I should choose another route. There are many buses I can take to school. Maybe she is all nice and lovely to me because she would like to eat me one day. I wouldn't want to be anybody's dish.

I just wish she would stop being kind to me. It is difficult to be rude to people that show you goodwill, isn't it? Anyway, I will try...

Today is the day. I decide to leave earlier than usual. I want to catch the 7:30 bus that stops near the supermarket where we buy snacks at breaktime. I walk faster than usual. I am feeling tense. If only I could be in my classroom right now. I am just confused.

There many people in the street already. Some of the faces are familiar. I shout out '*Sharp!*' from time to time. My curt greeting is returned with a '*Bho, bho* my friend!" None of this gives me pleasure. I feel extremely tense. Each step I take draws me closer to the bus stop. I think I will make it. I want to make it.

"It looks like you want to take a different bus today."

The voice is familiar. I hear it every day when I am going to school. I wish I had never heard that voice before. It sounds nice but today it carries a different meaning. Without looking back, I start running. I run as fast as my heels can carry me. My limbs are light and they do not betray me. I arrive safely at school. I recount the story of my survival. My classmates are stunned.

"We told you!' they finally say.

The next day, I go to school with Limbani. We take yet another route. We do not meet the old lady. Gradually, I start forgetting her.

"She must be dead by now," Limbani says. "We can try the old route just to see if she is still around."

Unfortunately, she is. She smiles at us when she sees us.

"Good morning my sons," she says.

"Good morning …*ago…go*," I stutter.

"Good morning old witch," Limbani shouts. "Leave us alone or my father will deal with you. Do you want to see what shaved the guinea fowl?"

I am shocked by Limbani's words. It is not good to talk to elderly people in such a way. No one has seen the old witch at her 'job' after all. It is not a crime to be childless, I think. I come to my senses.

"Don't mind him *agogo*. My friend didn't sleep well last night."

She is crying. You can read the hurt in her eyes.

"Crocodile tears!" Limbani blurts out jagged words.

"I wish you were kinder to me. I am just a lonely woman. I don't know what wrong I have done to you or your friends, but please forgive me."

"Goodbye *agogo*," I say. "I am afraid we will miss our bus. Take good care of yourself and don't mind us."

"Oh, I am sorry my sons for keeping you for so long. Your teachers won't be happy. What lovely boys you are… now hurry up, my sons. You don't want to miss your bus, do you?"

When Lions Come to Town

(with Adverbs of Time)

My grandfather says that fear is a wild animal that you create in your head.

"You should take a stick and chase it if you don't want it to pester you," he often tells me when I am scared in the middle of the night and I run to him for comfort.

"Go back to bed and don't be afraid of things that don't exist. Now let me sleep."

I eventually mumble an apology to *sekuru* and drag my feet to my room. The bed always looks sinister and I make it a point to sleep on the floor.

Sometimes, I get so scared and I become sweaty. Shadows lurk in the dark and I just cannot think straight. I try to be brave like *sekuru* and I never run to him again.

Later, when things get really bad, I imagine what I will do the following day with my best friend, Limbani. His name means 'be strong' in our Chichewa language and I want to be so strong that the lion in my head will take fright and escape. He will be so surprised of my strength that he will take flight like the *impalas* he usually hunts in the wilderness.

Limbani will be proud of me too. He is a good friend and I look up to him. We play together all the time when we are not at school. His parents own a grocery store. From time to time, his father gives us sweets when we run different kinds of errands for him. Occasionally, he makes us work with him in the store. It is generally a privilege and customers are surprised to see us counting well and giving the correct change. We rarely make mistakes.

Today, I have a master plan because I am fed up of being constantly harassed by the lion in my sleep. Moreover, grandfather has had enough of me bursting into his room, shouting as if a pride of lions were on my heels.

Therefore, tonight, I will not be taken unawares. They say that the best defence is attack. I am not afraid now. If the lion thinks I am weak and he can just pick on me, he will be in for a big surprise. It will surely remind him of this African proverb: *If you think you are too small to make a difference you haven't spent a night with a mosquito.*

If the lion comes after me tonight, I'll be like a mosquito.

First, I have already prepared a pack of books that I have placed on my bedside table. I will read these until I feel sleepy enough to turn off the lights. The lion only makes his visits in the dark because he is afraid of the light.

Secondly, I have put the biggest stick I could find in one corner of the room. If he sees me branding it, he will be scared and he will bolt for his life.

Next, if sticks don't scare him, I have a torch that I will turn on as soon as he tries to attack me. Lions cannot stand brightness. This will scare him off and he will never think of stepping into my house again.

Finally, I know that if everything does not work according to my plan, I can always go to grandfather. He is courageous, despite his old age, and he will keep me safe. He **ALWAYS** does.

And thinking of it, lions don't really come to town, do they? They stay in the jungle and do not visit human beings willy-nilly.

My lion will stay home with his family tonight and I will sleep like a baby.

The Most Beautiful Garden

(with Superlatives)

Everyone agrees this is the most beautiful garden. Only one person knows how long this garden has been here.

He tells anyone who wants to hear the story. We believe him because he is the oldest man in our village.

The story never gets old though. It is one of the best and most fascinating stories I've ever heard. I guess you are curious and you want to know what it is about.

Once upon a time there was a very rich family in this same village. They were not the wealthiest people in the country but they had a lot of land and cattle. Their food baskets were the fullest and their clothes were made from the most colourful and expensive fabrics any one could get.

However, they were not happy. In fact, they were the unhappiest family in the village and no one could understand.

Isn't their property enough to make them cheerful?

They walked about with slumped shoulders and sad eyes. No laughter came out of their mouths and no joy could be seen in their home. Their conversations were dull and full of melancholy.

One day, the head of the family decided to do something about their problem. He called his younger brother.

"My dear brother Misozi, listen to me. I think I've found the solution to our troubles."

"Do not tell me that Mavuto. Our problems are the worst in the whole world and we will never be able to solve them."

"This will work, believe me."

"I hope this will not turn out to be the craziest scheme you have ever come up with."

"Don't worry. Just wait and see. You will be the most surprised person in the entire universe."

The following day, Mavuto chose a piece of land not far from their house. It was dry and full of weeds. No one wanted to use it because it was difficult to tame.

"I will turn this into the most beautiful garden anyone has ever seen."

Like a mad man, he started digging and digging, removing stones and rubbish so as to prepare the ground for planting. He watered the ground every single day until it became soft and luscious. Soon, it was time to plant flowers, trees and vegetables.

His mood got better as time passed. He laughed more and his happiness was contagious. Later on, his wife and children joined and helped him to take care of the garden. What a sight! The complaints and fights had disappeared.

What remained was the loveliest family in the whole village. The children shrieked with unfettered joy and the adults no longer shouted at one another for no reason at all. It was the most beautiful thing to see.

A lot of time has passed since then. The old man says that the garden has been tended by at least three generations. Today, the family is not as affluent as it used to be. Rumour has it that they say that the garden is their most valuable possession. They take care of it as if it was an egg that could break at any moment.

The most beautiful garden in the village is the key to their happiness.

Beautiful Babies are Beautiful

(with Adjectives)

Tami and Talu are twins and they live in our street. They are very tall and talkative. This is why it hard to miss them. Think of it: two people that look alike and they tower over every single body. How can you not see them? Not seeing them is an impossible task.

Tami and Talu are two handsome young men who know how to talk to young women. They treat girls with respect and this is what girls like—to be treated with respect at all times. The twins know how to do this and they are treated well in return.

Tami and Talu were once beautiful babies. Everyone in our neighbourhood knew them because they were a marvel to look at. They were big and tall, and healthy and everything. On top of that, their resemblance was a marvel to look at. Tami and Talu made their mother very proud.

Tami and Talu's mother is still proud of her twins. They are two strong young men who never talk back to her with disrespect. Besides, they make her laugh and help her with many household tasks every single day. Those two boys can even cook! What a blessing they are. Tami and Talu will make their future wives proud. Indeed, beautiful babies are beautiful.

Tami and Talu want to marry. They want to get out of their parents' home and start families of their own. First of all, they have to get jobs and have a stable income before they can have beautiful babies of their own. Their mother is not worried though and she knows that they will turn into beautiful fathers. These two future parents, her own sons, will make their own sons happy and proud.

Tami and Talu are two proud young men. They work hard every single day and they make the most of their time. Most of all, they never bother anyone because they have no time to waste. You can almost read this on their foreheads:

TEAM TAMI AND TALU—Twins with a beautiful future and no time to waste.

Take it or leave it, jealous down. When I see Tami and Talu, I see the future of all our young men—young, beautiful and strong men; men with beautiful spirits and beautiful bodies; men with beautiful desires for the future.

Tami and Talu are beautiful young men with a beautiful future. I see nothing else.

Eight Days Before Christmas

(with Christmas Vocabulary)

The clock reads a quarter past seven.

My boss gave me a letter yesterday. He said I should open it eight days before Christmas. I don't know if it is a pay rise or simply a letter of dismissal. You never know with these people.

This is why I haven't read it yet. I know that my mood can be affected in two extreme ways. I will read it when I'm sure that I can handle its contents.

I am now going to work. The traffic is very busy. I feel tired but I do not let the general atmosphere affect me. It is easy to get upset in these conditions. The cars are moving like snails and you can see the other drivers getting impatient with each passing second.

I turn on the radio and look for music stations. There are mostly Christmas adverts: where to buy the best toys; where to get the finest food; where to spend Christmas Eve if you plan to go somewhere. I listen, my eyes set on the road in front of me.

Sometimes I cast an occasional glance at the sidewalks. They are teeming with different kinds of people. Most of the are like me: middle-aged, male, weary and heading towards unwelcoming workplaces.

I see a few students too. They have faces that are beaming with unexpected joy. Is it the festive season? Are they happy because they will be on holiday soon? Have they recently passed an exam? Are they looking forward to get the latest i-Phone or i-Pad? They look happy, I must say. I envy their nonchalance. I envy their spirited gaits and youthful expectation.

Decorations have been installed and I am sure that at night they must be a pretty sight. There are fairy lights of course and garlands made from real fir trees. The baubles are colourful and spectacular. There are all sorts of ornaments on shop windows. They look inviting and welcoming.

I remember that I have to buy my children Christmas presents. My son wants the latest PlayStation and my daughter wants a professional microphone to record her songs. I will buy perfume for my wife. I have no idea what I will get for myself. Maybe I should wait until I read the letter. If it's good news, I might spend more money. If it's bad news, then budget adjustments need to be made. Little food will be bought; cheap wine will grace our dinner table; fruits will be our perfect dessert and nothing will be allowed to go to waste.

After one hour and forty-five minutes, I reach my office building. All my colleagues but one have already arrived. We have an open space configuration and you can almost see what everybody is doing. I walk sheepishly to my desk and start working immediately. My boss sees me arriving of course. I hope this is not an excuse for him to fire me.

In the evening, I ostentatiously leave one hour later than everybody else to make up for the time I lost this morning. When I am leaving, I see a fake Father Christmas passing by with a bag full of things. He is thin and his beard is almost dropping from his droopy face.

I am happy that my son did not see him because he still believes that there is man who pays us a visit each Christmas Eve. He, and not me, is the one that gives him toys if he has been nice and well-behaved during the year.

I arrive home late. My wife has almost finished preparing dinner and the kids are watching TV. I go straight to the bedroom to drop my briefcase.

"Have you finally read the letter?" My wife asks me as soon as I join her in the kitchen. She gives me a small kiss on my forehead.

"No, not yet," I reply. " I will read it when the right time arrives."

"I don't know why someone would do something like that. Why can't he just tell you to read the letter whenever you want? Everything will be settled then and we will stop being worried. Do you think it's a nice surprise?"

"I don't know really. It could be anything."

My wife hugs me and tells me that we will all be fine.

Time passes slowly and when then the fateful day arrives, I shiver with dreadful expectation. What is in the letter?

My wife asks if she can read it with me but I decline her thoughtful offer.

I close the bedroom door and sit on the bed. Carefully opening the envelop with my fingers and then a ruler, I start reading the letter:

Dear Mr. Christopher Bright,

I am pleased to announce that we have decided to organise a Christmas party for the children of our employees this year.

It is my pleasure to inform you that you will be our first Father Christmas.

We will provide you with more details regarding the organisation of this exceptional event.

Wishing you all the best.
Sincerely,
Jack Robinson

Ha, ha, ha, the nerve of him!

I went out of the bedroom and announced the good news to my wife. She heaved a sigh of relief, of course, and vowed that she would take a lot of pictures of me. You don't get to see your husband dressed as Father Christmas every day of the week!

Rambo

(with Vocabulary for
Talking about People)

Today we have a meeting with Rambo after school. We don't really want to see him because he scares us a lot. My friend Justin says we should go straight home because Rambo is double trouble.

I tell Justin that Rambo will beat us up if we don't do what he wants.

"Do you remember the last time he slapped your older brother, Edson, on his way to school because he didn't say hi to him?"

Justin remembers of course! We talked about the incident for days. Actually, Edson had to appease Rambo's anger with fried chicken a and a bottle of cold Coca-Cola.

This is why I don't want to make Rambo angry. It's never good to make Rambo angry. Things never end well with him.

Justin is adamant though. He insists that we should go home anyway.

"If we keep on doing what Rambo wants, he'll never stop his bad behaviour. We have to stand up to him. I don't want to live in fear all my life."

He adds that a slap is a slap and it never killed anyone. What's bad is to be scared of Rambo all the time.

"Charles, you can't do whatever you want because you're always afraid of him. Who's Rambo anyway? He's just a boy! He's got two legs and two arms just like you! We have to be strong Charles."

I think about what Justin has just said. He's right. If we keep rewarding Rambo with our fear, he'll never stop. We therefore decide to be brave. We'll go home without seeing him. Period.

As soon as the bell rings, we take our bags and scramble out of the classroom. We were supposed to meet Rambo at the tuck shop but we decide not to go there. On our way back, we're very scared but we don't see Rambo.

I'm so happy when I reach home. I tell my brothers what just happened.

"What?" they ask me, their voices filled with terror. "You decided to defy Rambo!"

Suddenly my body is filled with dread and I start trembling.

"Charles is going to be beaten up tomorrow! Charles is going to be beaten up tomorrow!" my brothers chant and I now realise that I should have gone to see Rambo at the tuck shop instead of going back home like a coward.

My younger brother sees how worried I am and he tries to comfort me in his own way.

"Don't worry Charles. I'll lend you my slingshot so that you can defend yourself against him."

I think that's a very bad idea.

My elder brother Michael adds that I should put a few stones in my schoolbag in case Rambo tries to give me trouble the following day. Maybe I might do that. I don't have to use the stones though, I tell myself.

At night, I have awful nightmares and I'm so glad to wake up the following morning. I barely touch my breakfast and my mother asks me why I'm not eating. I tell her that I'm not hungry.

"Can I take your bread?" Michael asks me and I start giving it to him when my mother stops me.

"Take it to school Charles. You can't study on an empty belly."

I listen to her advice and take the bread with me even though I really don't feel like filling my belly right now. I wonder how I'm going to survive the day.

When I arrive at school, I don't see Rambo. As a matter of fact, I don't want to see him at all. Justin comes to see me at break time and he tells me that he heard that Rambo is looking for us.

"Is he angry?" I ask Justin.

"What do you think?" Justin replies and I say nothing.

During the day we're really afraid and we don't go out of the classroom in case we meet Rambo. Actually, the trick works like magic because we don't meet Rambo for at least four days. Yeah!

However, one day when we're going back home, we meet Rambo. He's alone and he looks really cross.

Rambo is very tall, dark-skinned and muscular. He often wears a pair of black boots to add to his threatening

look. His eyes are always red because he smokes mari-
juana. Well, that's what my classmates say.

"Justin, do you see what I see?" I ask, my voice shaking.

My friend doesn't answer but starts running back
where we came from. I have no time to react. My legs are
wobbly and they refuse to carry my frame. I just freeze
where I'm standing. When I look back, Justin is nowhere
to be seen. However, Rambo *has* seen me. Oh, that's bad
news. Besides, he looks happy. He really looks happy to
see me. Maybe he's thinking "Today I'm going to teach
that boy a lesson!"

He walks towards me, taking his time. When he finally
reaches where I am, he asks me why I didn't go to see him
the other day at the tuck shop."

"I don't …know," I mumble a reply.

"Do you know who I am?" he throws me another
question.

"I know who you are, of course. Rambo, I have a question for you though. Is your real name Rambo? It's because
you don't look like him. You know the real Rambo in the
film. He has long hair and you don't!"

Rambo stares at me as if I've just told him that he's a
girl. Then he starts laughing and touching his head which
has got short, frizzy hair.

"I don't need to have long hair to look like Rambo.
Look at me, I'm tall and muscular. I think that I can even
beat the real Rambo in a fight."

He sees my incredulous face.

"I can beat him. What's your name again little boy?"

"Charles," I answer him timidly.

"Charles, you see. I'm really strong. The problem is that Rambo lives so far away. I will never be able to meet him."

"That's true. I agree with you hundred percent. I think that you're very strong as well. I would love to see such a fight though."

"Really?" he asks me enthusiastically. "Do you think that I'm that strong? I could beat him, couldn't I?"

"Of course you could!"

He grins.

"You're very strong Rambo. You're actually stronger than the real Rambo."

I see him smiling some more and loosening up. His anger seems to be thawing.

"Why did your friend ran away? Is he afraid of Rambo?"

"I don't how," I smile. "I don't know why he ran away."

Rambo starts laughing like a mad person.

"Tell him not to be afraid of me next time. I don't bite."

I stay quiet and wait to see what Rambo will do next.

"Let me escort you home. What did you say your name was once again?"

"Charles."

"My dear Charles, don't worry. My name is Rambo. I'll take you home and no one will harm you."

We walk safely home.

(I won't tell you what my brothers said when they saw me walking with Rambo! □ □ □)

Tobias, the Houseboy

(with Vocabulary for Talking about Houseboys)

Tobias came to our house when I was nine years old . He was thin and short and my mother told us that he had come to work for us.

"Treat him with respect at all times. He has children who are as old as you are."

My mother advised us to call our 'servant' Uncle Tobias even though he was just a mere houseboy. We didn't understand why we were to call him 'Uncle' since we were not related to him. He even didn't come from the same village as my mother or father.

Uncle Tobias was supposed to take care of the house and cook for us. He was also instructed to take care of the front garden and water the vegetable plants that were in our backyard.

His tasks also included washing all our dirty clothes and plates, cleaning our dirty windows and cars and finally ironing the washed clothes and putting them away in our wardrobes.

In exchange, Uncle Tobias received a salary, left-over clothes, free food and free board. He was happy because he never went to bed on an empty stomach.

He even had some extra money and clothes to take back home once in a while. It was tough to get such a job in town so he took his responsibilities seriously.

We were therefore surprised when things started missing in our house.

"It's Uncle Tobias," my cousin who stayed with us said. "It can't be anyone else."

My pair of sneakers that my father had bought in South Africa the month before had gone missing. We also couldn't find my sister's denim skirt that she loved so much. Two of my father's shirts were nowhere to be seen. My mother complained that her two beloved *chitenjes* that had vanished as well.

We couldn't believe that Uncle Tobias was capable of stealing. He looked honest to me. My father said that the only way to know what had happened was to ask him.

My mother agreed and organised a meeting with Uncle Tobias. She asked him about the missing items and he said that he had not seen them. My mother threatened to take him to the Police station if the things did not reappear. However, Uncle Tobias maintained his position.

One item reappeared after that but, generally, the situation did not change. We still couldn't find our things and new items were added to the list of missing stuff. We were desperate and fed up.

My mother decided to confront our houseboy (or 'houseman' for that matter).

"ATobias, I'm really tired of this situation. I want to know here and today who exactly is taking our stuff. My husband and I work very hard for these things. You better have a good answer."

Like the first time, Uncle Tobias maintained his innocence and we didn't have any physical proof of his guilt so we let it go.

Uncle Tobias continued to work hard even though he knew that we all suspected that he was a notorious thief.

As for us, it was hard to respect somebody whom we thought was taking advantage of us.

One day, Uncle Tobias said that he had decided to go back to his hometown because he couldn't live in a house where everybody thought he was a thief.

We were all surprised but we decided to let him leave because we were convinced that he was stealing from us.

A few days later, we found a hole behind our house. Our dog had been digging it for days.

We inspected it and found the missing items there. You see, our dog was pregnant and was about to give birth soon! She was our culprit of course.

My mother was very emotional. She knew that Uncle Tobias had left our house because of our suspicion.

"We should do the right thing. We should bring back Uncle Tobias."

We all agreed and the following weekend, my father went to pick him up from his hometown.

Uncle Tobias couldn't believe his luck and he agreed to come back home right away!

When he arrived, we apologised to him and told him that things would be better for him. Uncle Tobias was happy.

Our dog gave birth to six cute puppies a few days later. We gave five away and kept one for us. We called the dog Tootsie because he is such a cute dog.

There are no more missing items now. At least, we don't lose them every day as it was in those early days.

Doggie the Dog

(with Vocabulary for Talking about Dogs)

My father wants to buy a dog so that he can guard the house. He wants to get a big, fierce dog that can bark at thieves and bite them if they try to steal from us.

There's a notorious robber who roams our neighbourhood day and night looking for things to pinch. We have to put all valuable things inside the house to keep them safe.

This is why a dog is going to be very useful to us, my father insists.

The problem is we don't really like dogs in our family. They are often thin and they don't always look nice. When they have wounds, flies hover about them and it's not a pleasant thing to see. They even smell bad sometimes.

It's therefore a big surprise when my father brings home a puppy.

"He's cute!" we all scream.

"I thought you didn't like dogs!" my father exclaims. "You see, I told you. It's not a bad idea to have a dog."

My father chose well. Doggie is beautiful. His fur is brown and he has got white spots here and there. His nose is small and black. He also has got big eyes and short ears.

When Doggie hears one of us coming, he wags his short, furry tail to show that he's happy. When it's somebody he doesn't know, he barks with his squeaky voice to warn us that there's an intruder.

As of now, he only drinks milk because he's too small. My father says that later, he will eat normal food like *nsima* and meat. My mother says that we shouldn't give him beans because he's going to fall sick. My father's right. Dogs who eat beans lose their fur and they have all sorts of diseases. They look very pitiful. I don't want Doggie to become like that.

Doggie is getting bigger. He now sleeps outside in a small wooden doghouse. A carpenter made it for us for a small fee. I painted it white with some paint I found in the house. The house looks cute. Doggie sleeps a lot during the day, but during the night he has to remain awake so that he can guard the house against ruthless thieves.

When he gets out of his doghouse, we put him on a leash. We attach him to a tree so that he cannot bite our friends or whoever visits our house. Doggie cannot go out of our compound on his own and we don't take him out for walks either because people are afraid that he will bite them.

Our friends' parents are worried that Doggie can have rabies and give it to their children. Rabies is a disease that's incurable. This is why we take him to the vet's every week so that he can stay healthy.

We love doing this every Saturday. The vet's very far and we have to go there on foot. Hence, on Friday, we go to bed very early and wake up at around half-past five the following morning. We go to the vet's with my friends and my brother.

The walk is always pleasant and we tell each other stories and jokes along the way. Sometimes we find wild fruit alongside the road. We always stop to eat some. We're very happy when we do.

There are always many people at the vet's. It's a big place that's full of big baths that are filled with products to protect dogs against ticks. Doggie barks a lot while he's bathing because he doesn't like the muddy water and the other dogs make him nervous too.

Sometimes, the vet also gives Doggie his vaccines and checks if he has any parasites on him. If he's sick, he gives him some medicine to get well. We are grateful to have such a vet because he's not expensive and he really takes good care of our dog.

We want to keep Doggie for a long time because our family loves him so much.

The Astronaut from Bolero
(with Space Vocabulary)

I decided to become an astronaut when I was four years old. It was a magazine clipping that triggered this passion for space. I am now fifteen years old and I still believe that I will be part of a spaceship crew one day.

In fact, I am not the only one to have such high ambitions. My best friend, Mwiza, is passionate about planes. He spends his free time making Boeing models that he sells to us. You will not see him wasting his energy on useless things because he wants to be a pilot in fifteen years' time. Fifteen years, not less, not more. He talks about this day in and day out. Aircrafts are his whole world.

My own brother wants to be a scientist. Each month, he invents plays in which someone from Bolero discovers the treatment for Aids or another incurable disease. We like his plays because they give us a lot of hope and strength. He has a special heart, my brother. He will do great things for us one day.

I should also mention Takondwa. We call her 'The Tomboy' because she is always fighting with us. She says that she is going to be an architect. She is really pretty and intelligent. I am sure she will transform Bolero into a five-star village and more than that. I know she will do it. Takondwa has a tough spirit.

We live by our passions. I have several pictures of telescopes, spaceships and space shuttles. You will see them on the walls of the bedroom I share with my two younger cousins. On the floor, I have a collection of space-related objects. One of them is a miniature of Jupiter planet that Mwiza gave me a year ago. I was so surprised when he showed me this that I could not speak for several minutes. In the end I cried because what he did was very beautiful.

Being an astronaut is all I ever think of. At night the stars seem very far but they still retain their shining beauty. I wonder how it would feel like to be near them, to touch them, to admire their radiance. I recently read about the man who walked on the moon. His surname is Armstrong, I have forgotten his first name. I even saw his photograph where he is dressed in what they call a space suit, I think. I will wear one of those one day, surely. I wonder what my mother will think of her handsome son :-))

Our teachers are always encouraging us to think of the impossible. They stretch our minds and horizons. My favourite subject is Geography. The teacher is a walking encyclopaedia, I tell you. We are all fascinated by what he knows about faraway countries, but it is his jokes we love the most. If he catches you dozing off in class, he screams at the top of his voice, calling your name: " Wake up Vitumbiko! The Express bus for Blantyre is leaving without you!" You can imagine the culprits' reactions and our hilarity! We cannot stop laughing in Mr. Nyirenda's class.

Next month, I will no longer be in Bolero. I have to go to a better secondary school in Lilongwe. I will live with my mother's brother, Mr. Kayira. He works as an accountant in a bank. He is very hardworking and thoughtful so I do not want to disappoint him by being careless. His wife is also very kind. She is a Science and Mathematics teacher- what a nice surprise! I will learn as much as I can from her.

My future guardians stay in Kawale, in a three-bedroom house with running water and built-in toilets. They even have a fridge and a cooker. It will be a big change from my life here. Forget the paraffin, forget the candles- I will be able to read as many books as I want at night thanks to the electricity. I will have no excuses if I fail. Mr Nyirenda warned us anyway-"If he catches one of us on a lousy job in the future, he will drag us back to school, even if we have our own children or we are sporting gray hair on our heads!". I think he was not joking this time.

I am going to miss my family and friends a lot. It is the price to pay for my burning ambitions. I will come back here though. I cannot imagine staying away from my place of birth forever. I will come back to see Mwiza and Mr. Nyirenda. I will come back to be with my old and well-deserving parents. By then, they will be calling me 'the Astronaut from Bolero'. To say the truth, I will not mind this nickname. Not at all. Not for a single second!

Dreams Can't Be Too Big

(with Motivation Vocabulary)

You're going to Blantyre Secondary School."

I cannot believe the news. I am finally going to my school of choice!

"You deserve it my son."

My mother is weeping but her tears are of joy. She is happy for me, and proud- I can it see it from the way she keeps on straightening my collar.

"We have to buy new clothes for you."

"Don't bother yourself *wâmama*. I'm only going to Blantyre after all!"

"To the city you mean. I don't want my son to fail because he didn't have any decent clothes. You will have two new pairs of trousers and three shirts, not forgetting the uniform."

I open my mouth to protest but my father and mother will hear none of it. They are strong, my parents, they are. They work hard for me, for us, for everyone in the family. They really want us to succeed.

It was not easy to get the money for my school fees, but they managed. I see the strain in their weary eyes, on their hunched backs, in their tired legs. You will not hear them complaining though. Never. They say that complaints never fed anyone in this world. You have to wake up in the morning and do everything you can to live a dignified life. 'Dignity' is my father's favourite word. You can be poor but that does not mean the world has to see your misery.

This is why we are always dressed in clean and well-mended clothes. We also put on shoes all the time. Our hair is always combed. No, you will not see us walking in rags. We wake up early in the morning to sweep our yard and our house. We take great care of ourselves and our environment because we know that it is necessary. It is necessary to love ourselves and where we live. We can be poor but we do not have to look poor. This is how we triumph over our circumstances.

My parents say we have to keep on dreaming. If we wallow in our misery, we will never get out of this place. We have to look farther than the horizon, higher than the sky, deeper than the lake. Our possibilities are endless, they insist. We are going to make it.

I have big dreams. My dreams are so big that they sometimes keep me awake at night. I know that I will achieve them, of course, I will. It is no use to have dreams if you cannot do anything about them. My mother says what matters is the purpose. "Dream my children, dream," she often tells us. " You can be anything you want in this world, you can be anything. Don't be afraid, be strong. Be strong my children and work towards your dreams." I love my parents, I really do. I will make them very happy one day, I will really do.

What are my dreams? Not only do I want to be a surgeon, I also want to be one of the best surgeons in my country. I know I will make it, I will. I will work hard, every single day of my life, I will.

Why do I want to be a surgeon? I could be somebody else: a businessman, a lawyer, a judge, a politician, whatever. No, I want to be a doctor who heals people. I want to see people happy. I want to see people realising their dreams. I want to see sorrow become a thing of the past.

During those restless nights, I think of my future, of what I will become, of what I will do. I picture myself receiving my final degree. I just cannot wait. This is what enables me to get out of bed at sunrise. I have so much energy, I do not know what to do with it!

When I have finished helping my parents with their chores, I sit down under the shade of our precious mango tree and then I read. I read until I cannot read any more. I read everything I can get my hands on. Each time I finish a book, I know I am getting closer to my dream.

Being selected to Blantyre Secondary School is just the first step to my bright future. My parents will no longer suffer, I promise them, they never will.

THE END